IRRESISTIBLE

poems by

Lynne Burnett

Finishing Line Press
Georgetown, Kentucky

IRRESISTIBLE

Copyright © 2018 by Lynne Burnett
ISBN 978-1-63534-442-4 First Edition
All rights reserved under International and Pan-American Copyright Conventions. No part of this book may be reproduced in any manner whatsoever without written permission from the publisher, except in the case of brief quotations embodied in critical articles and reviews.

ACKNOWLEDGMENTS

Grateful acknowledgment is made to the following publications in which these poems previously appeared:

Calyx Journal: "After The Paper Folds Shut" and "Irreplaceable"
Geist: "Hunter and Ziggy"
IthacaLit: "Tandem Hang-Gliding Incident" (Winner of the 2016 Lauren K. Alleyne Difficult Fruit Poetry Prize) and "Guy Climbs Mount LaFayette Feb. 6, 2000"
Malahat Review: "On Hearing That A Friend's Husband Died In His Sleep"
New Millennium Writings, 25th Anthology: "Miracle"
North Shore Magazine: "Raccoon"
Pandora's Collective: "Morning Blessing" (Winner of the 2012 Spring Poetry Contest)
Taos Journal of International Poetry & Art: "It Rains For Him"
Tupelo Press Chapbook Anthology: "Mute With Thanks"
The Ultra Best Short Verse Anthology: "On My Neighbour's Removal Of A Beautiful Tree"

Publisher: Leah Maines
Editor: Christen Kincaid
Cover Art: Stewart Burnett
Author Photo: Stewart Burnett
Cover Design: Elizabeth Maines McCleavy

Printed in the USA on acid-free paper.
Order online: www.finishinglinepress.com
also available on amazon.com

Author inquiries and mail orders:
Finishing Line Press
P. O. Box 1626
Georgetown, Kentucky 40324
U. S. A.

Table of Contents

Glass Slippers 1

Tandem Hang-Gliding Incident 2

After The Paper Folds Shut 3

Guy Climbs Mount LaFayette Feb. 6, 2000 4

On Hearing That A Friend's Husband Died In His Sleep 5

Irresistible 6

Legacy 7

Irreplaceable 9

Night's Good Pupil 10

Sharm El-Sheikh, Egypt 11

This Water Knows 12

Fishing Lodge, Hakai Pass 13

Seal Pup, Homfray Channel 14

Raccoon 15

Hunter And Ziggy, ... 16

Against Certainty 17

On My Neighbour's Removal Of A Beautiful Tree 18

Miracle 19

Mute With Thanks 20

It Rains For Him, ... 21

Morning Blessing 22

Such A Blue 23

After A Health Scare 24

Jane Kenyon Lives Again 25

Date Night 26

*for my family—all of you—
near and far*

GLASS SLIPPERS

Walking barefoot
across the dewy lawn,
the grass riotous with light
that began its journey toward her
over four billion years ago,
light that will burn five billion
years more after she's gone,

like candle to candle lit
my pixie daughter's a thirsty wick
for joy, sure any life glad to be
is all that matters,
and I want to tell her *yes*

while light is leading her heart
out its small window
of time, and blade by blade
from beaded grass her
own glass slippers made,
yes
before gravity weighs in.

TANDEM HANG-GLIDING INCIDENT

An anniversary gift, her first time doing it
Lenami Godinez-Avila, 27, hugged the pilot
from behind as instructed, ran with him
awkwardly to the edge and stepped
into the wind-tug beyond anyone's reach—

her harness not clipped on. She fell
like Icarus a thousand feet, melting
from sight with the pilot's shoes
into a sea of limbs webbed with leaves
down, down to the forest floor.

Her boyfriend, filming it,
stopped. Love screamed
through the air as he ran down
Mt. Woodside to find her.
Until he did, there was hope.

The pilot glided back to an open
mouthed crowd, to his twelve
year old daughter watching,
and swallowed the memory
card onboard. His fiftieth birthday.

Who hasn't known each of them
in dreams?—where we fall without
falling, see what can't be happening,
get to creatively escape a bad scene.
And wake relieved, our lives still

hanging by a thread of assumptions.

AFTER THE PAPER FOLDS SHUT
The Vancouver Sun, June 3rd, 2008

On opposite pages of the newspaper,
the black and white of two headlines
face each other: "Teacher Leaves
Children Behind in Quake" and "Hero
Died Saving Others From Grenade."

Villain could have been hero,
hero as easily villain,
in the split second each had
to choose between all for one
and one for all.

Until that moment is ours, it's a phantom
reminder that we don't really know
on what side of the fence we'd fall.
Either way—casualties, long after
the paper folds shut: I think of all

the mothers the teacher didn't,
their anger mixing with tears,
and of his wife and small daughter,
now looking at him
from across the chasm of doubt,

and of the hero, a fresh nineteen like my son,
and of the hero's mother, not saved
from that grenade, having the unfathomable
task of praising her son for his last breath,
then mourning him until hers.

GUY CLIMBS MOUNT LAFAYETTE FEB. 6, 2000

Unlike other guys
who reach a mountaintop and leave with it, move it
under the hut of the body
so they can breathe its rare air at will,
see themselves later through anything,

Guy Waterman got stuck on one craggy point
that jagged heaven: it put the bit in his mouth
he could speak to God only there,
called it his kind of prayer. And so his rosary
of left foot, right foot began, decades
of climbing the same mountain, breaking
out of the fog and cloud into a brilliance
of mind and sky. Each time harder to take
lucky boots and crampons off, wear ordinary
shoes: where they tread, a son leaves, is
never seen or heard from again; others die.

Each son lost thickening the Gordian
knot of unspeakable sorrow. How possibly
deter him from wanting to freeze in time
a transcendent moment of no return?
Love stayed his wife: at home, knowing.
Praying for a below zero night. And so
he stepped onto the Old Bridle Path,
nodding his last hello at Agony Ridge,
a few hikers headed down before the sun set.
Had a canteen half-water, half-alcohol.
Had a wind that took his breath away.

Not turning back, instead turning his back
on this world, he struck his father's
wooden alpenstock into the ice five feet
off the trail and curled up beside it,
placing a period where the small comma
of his body would be seen. Three days passed
before friends muscled him down on a stretcher
for what felt like forever. Finally was.

ON HEARING THAT A FRIEND'S HUSBAND DIED IN HIS SLEEP

Death's an increasingly regular face
in our crowd, mostly dropping by
unannounced, such that I, too, might
turn over one morning, prompted awake
by Brother Jake on our favourite rock
radio station and find you smiling, your
eyes still closed, and nestling my head
as usual into your armpit and laying
my left arm across your belly,
fall through the ice
of a body devoid of breath,
and wonder what bad dream this is.

Forgive me for thinking then of your
Achilles heel—your feet so sensitive,
no one can touch them. For three
decades, just the dare of my hand
hovering over an exposed foot has
got you up and running. I confess to
imagining your eventual acquiescence
as a deliberate act of love to me some
wine-deep night on holiday. Not me
frantically rubbing your feet, rubbing
them like magic lamps, wishing
I couldn't.

IRRESISTIBLE
> "Bride Drowns While Modelling Wedding Gown Near Rawdon"
> CTV News Montreal—Aug. 24, 2012

First a coquettish dip of toes in the shallows, then a saucy
wade, the mud bottom making it easy to balance.

The Oureau River glinting, hurrying out of sight. Just Maria
and the photographer, before she consigned the dress to a box.

What next but to lift her veil, unmoor a few minds?—
swim a little, where it was deeper…not knowing

how thirsty that dress was: how it would drink and drink
and drink, until its weight was unbearable,

no Houdini to hold open the elevator door long enough
to uncuff her from all the snug finery, the lacy squeeze

of her lungs, irresistible pull to the river's bed.
How her heart surely sank before she did, gonging

regret and betrayal. Sounds like a Stephen King story—
a gown with vows of its own. No, the horror's more

the slippery ease with which vanity slides under our skin,
looks in the mirror, one way or another does us in.

LEGACY

At the dinner party, eleven people,
not twelve.
A striking redhead, warmly smiling—
the one whose world had recently halved.
Those of us who didn't know
wouldn't have known.

I'm used to death
ringing a bell that won't stop
singing of loss as love's
forgotten child—a call to mass
sung down the long corridors
of bone.

The mouth that can hush it
speaks to me
of a love built brick by brick,
circling a great and dangerous fire,
holding that heat
like a hand to the heart
when only ash is left.

Has lips full of secret amens,
stretching a smile beyond
mere courtesy, until it cracks
me open, I who have not
yet travelled that road
or those blurred miles from home.

Night falls before we know it:
death has a thing for a man about
to retire. Like a virus, it jumps
from acquaintance to friend to kin,
no sympathy for women and children.
Taking on mass and weight, given

a name, it terribly crowds a room.
This being human—to matter.
Through our bodies. Past them.
Her smile all I can see
of love's fierce alchemy—bright
crack of light escaping a closed door.

IRREPLACEABLE

My father had the good fortune
to be visited by six women
last Friday: Carol came to clean
his house, do laundry, get the mail,
Sue to bathe him, then cook lunch
and dinner, Ann to cut his gnarly
toe nails and massage his feet, Barb—
a nurse—to check his vitals, Louise
to tame his dead wife's garden, and
Lynne, his daughter from three thousand
miles away, to make sure he was okay.

The door kept opening, we came
and went, and the golden October
light wandered from room to room,
like us, not in a hurry to leave. And he
glowed with the attention, feasting on
a cornucopia of witty conversation
through the rise and fall of our busy hands,
we, the chance wives of widower row.
But come darkness across the sheets
of his bed, we were all forgotten as he
patted the spot beside him, whispering
"Night-night, love"—as he always had—
to the irreplaceable one.

NIGHT'S GOOD PUPIL

Variable, the pastures hooved by lives
in full gallop, unbridled by time:
beneath the immutable drift of the sun
move the rounded and risen,
the angled and gleaming, the limbs,
wings, fins sweating with use.
Unstoppably given to their one life.

As the light gives unstoppably—
teacupped in petals, glowing
in a green persuasion of leaves,
slipping through salt-licked grains
of sand, lifted high on a spread
wing, in the flash and splash
of a salmon's fin, between a deer's
leap and a dog's outstretched paw.

And this, the monopoly of earth's
home star: a bright creeping
into the rooms behind closed doors.
This is night's good pupil, daily bent
over the riveting texts of our world,
whose gaze, upon turning
a sudden last page, stays warm
on the straightening back of a man,
warm on his unstoppable hands.

SHARM EL-SHEIKH, EGYPT

In the newspaper, a photo of a youth
taking the picture of a young couple
standing in front of the once beautiful
Ghazala Gardens Hotel:
the man, shielded
from the sun by dark glasses,
arms loose at his side,
the woman, lion-maned,
her tawny bare belly sliding out
from a spotless white pleated skirt,

both smiling those postcard
"Wish You Were Here" smiles
as if the building behind them
had not, overnight, been destroyed
by a bomb,
as if lives as innocent as theirs
had not been lost,
as if, when on vacation
one must go on
having a good time.

Or as if, having safely emerged
from the shadowy remains
of a Red Sea resort
that lived up to its name,
behind the shining columns
of the bared teeth
of their smiles,
they cannot hear
other carefully constructed
worlds collapsing.

THIS WATER KNOWS

Below this whale song of waves: the fin-happy,
sounding through all the dumb canyons
of the sea, coloured crayon-bright in the dark
flooded basement of the earth, shadow-drifted
across aqueous meadows prismed with light,
blending with gray rock and white sand,
knobby coral and long swishy green,
ferned and prickled, smoothed and elongated,
troubled hard, dense, small

but here, and free—
the mute-mouthed, mandibled hungry
and the hunted—to a grotto-chased,
honorable death. Or those given eyes
to see the dangling hook, the silver
door swinging shut before it's too late.
Those at least, weapons in the hand.
Not a cavernous ground zero.
Not here.

But this water knows, in its reach, how
my bikini got its name. Makes me think
of dreams I barely had, so quickly did they
sink from sight, but whose notes floated
long after, as if there was something
I could yet retrieve. In a tidal lullabye
of voices I cannot hear, the many mouths
of the sea open and close, open and close
lips I cannot read.

FISHING LODGE, HAKAI PASS

Early morning
with the precision of birds
the fishermen go out,
slickered and keen-eyed,
hands on the rudder
of the rest of their lives.

Every day, kings
and drama queens get
pulled from their kingdoms,
gasp against fiberglass,
get bonked on the head,
don't know what hit them.

Early evening, the beaten
and the just plain beat
line up on the long dock
until the last rod-wrestler
weighs in with his picture
perfect catch,

hanging from
that stainless steel hook
a stilled, still shining body
whose open eyes stare back
from a height never imagined.
Sweet Jesus, Jack!

SEAL PUP, HOMFRAY CHANNEL

A searing yowl from the rocky shore.
Again.   Again.   Stops all conversation
in the dinghy and we motor closer.
A lone seagull is waiting for its prize,
flanked by a dozen seals draped over
the surrounding rocks. The gull flies off
at our approach and the seals slip frantically
from their posts into the murmurring sea,
leaving one black cigar shape well above the tideline
still breathing in the bright promise of another day:

it's a seal pup, eyes oozing oceans
of green and yellow pus. He lifts a flipper
as I tip a bucket of saltwater gently over him
and then, lips curling, sausages himself
between two rocks. I try pouring the water
over the rocks to drip down on him but
unable to wriggle any further away,
he turns his head, teeth bared.
There'll be no mothering for this
fast-aging, whiskered face:

he will live unassisted
until the life he was given is taken back,
until the blazing August light becomes a second skin
and the lapping sounds of rising water carry him
off into the salmon-glinting sea of his birth,
until death, not taken from him,
death is all his,
rendering the blurred shapes that swam
once beside him—nothing more
than an unfinished dream.

RACCOON

Mid-morning along the winding coastal road,
snout pressed to the pavement: a large raccoon.
No swerving—I stop and pick it up
with an old towel from the trunk of the car.
It is heavy, striped fur soft, still warm,
little hands so like mine.

Carefully I lay the body in a ditch
thick with the honeyed leaves of autumn
for I, too, want to die untrampled.
Turning to go, I see a family
of eyes intently watching
from the light-soaked foliage
on the other side of the road,
eyes that look directly into mine.

Like any good mother, she led the way,
taking the unstoppable car's blow,
last night's quiet masked bandit,
locked out of our world, shuffling
empty-handed back into hers,
heaped love that padded by, unrevered,
whose conversation with this earth
is now done, opening wide
the mouths of her young.

HUNTER AND ZIGGY,

a rascally lab-shepherd
and grumpy old cat
didn't much like each other;
both bristled to share
the same family,
same house.

After the fire,
finding them:
curled up—
for the first time,
together—
under the upstairs rug,

the cat that couldn't
swat death away,
gathered into
the dog's clumsy paws.

AGAINST CERTAINTY
for Brenda

I saw you early today in the window
of your den that overlooks the street,

no doubt googling the latest treatment
options in a blur, while a Howe Sound

wind held office among the skyscraping
trees, rifling through the leaves like it

was looking for something, someone
and I dared to hope that far from the

finality of a label, written or spoken,
your body could soar in the open air

of its dreaming places and be nameless,
ageless, free again of any diagnosis, and

that behind the pane you too could hear
birds now shuffling through their notes

as if in concert with lifting the dark
sentence from that tiny cell of a word.

ON MY NEIGHBOUR'S REMOVAL OF A BEAUTIFUL TREE

that spoiled his view of the ocean:
the tree had the last word,
ending its considerable life
with the Chekhovian grin
of a hole in the ground
that shouted and shouted
until my neighbour
running, heard.

MIRACLE

Is it a miracle
that I found the worm in time—
having gone into my den much earlier
than usual, to turn the computer on—
and saw the dark, exhausted thread of its
body lying in the middle of a desert
of beige carpet, picked it up, barely moist, and
laid it outside on the wet grass, and watched
until it finally waved goodbye at one end,
easing itself into the darkness it knows?

Or is the miracle
that the annelid slid
through sealed doors and windows
to get inside my house in the first place,
that it became a finger pointing
from the Buddha's hand,
laying at my feet its five paired hearts
and the power of intervention—
of life continued
or of death without comment?

Is there a day without its miracle,
for doesn't one follow the other
because of a vast accordion of worms
playing now the soil's anthem, now its dirge,
burrowing through millennial darknesses
so plants can breathe and grow, and
become the planet's green lungs feeding
the body of this world, each inhabitant
still part of that first inspiration:
the good air of life lived, wholly inspired.

MUTE WITH THANKS

Had she jumped with him
from their small boat
into those wind-walling waves
in the Bay of Banderas,
to cool off that cloudless afternoon—
like he asked, like they'd done before—
long-marrieds straddling sixty:
he in his element, proud swimmer
reborn every hot holiday,
and she, fearful of surf, actually preferring
the freefall into deep water;

had she also been fooled
by the wind—travelling a whole knot
faster than they thought, making
any progress incremental, quickly lost,
no matter one's muscle or desire—
the boat slowly drifting away
until he had to tread water,
water too deep to anchor in,
water slapping his face,
no one else in sight and he
like a man betrayed, frowning;

had she said *yes* feeling *no*,
who could have asked the next question?—
and start the engine
when he nodded in disbelief,
backing up the boat until the swim ladder
was within reach, and as the water surged
and pushed him hard against it, help
pull him sputtering from the great
mother sea, naked as at birth,
and wrap him in a towel, her arms.
Suddenly as old as their children
already thought they were.

IT RAINS FOR HIM,

who loves it more than sunshine,
the streets so wet tonight, they are tongues
babbling in the dark—glossolalia—
they gleam baptismal, it's like
the slosh of good wine in the mouth,
how many ways can it be praised? and
how auspicious!—easier to leave the house
he was born in twenty-one years earlier
when drop by drop it taps on every window
calling his name, and out he goes for a walk
(like having a bath sprinkled with Dead
Sea salts, he can't help but wallow in it)
such a glad soak, hair dripping, shoes
squishing already reaching the corner
and look, the light is with him,
the interminable traffic has stopped,
the next step beckons—that wide avenue
known to swallow a man whole—
now's when a mother crosses
her fingers—momentum will carry him
curb after curb walking on water like this.

MORNING BLESSING

One large glass of water daily
before the endless cups of green tea,

a glass that stood wrapped
a long time in my father's two hands,

head bowed to it, eyes closed
to the rest of us at the table.

I didn't know what he thought
or felt or said to himself right then

nor how thirsty I was
for a silence so *meant*

until I felt it filling me too,
slaking the cracked creekbed

of rushed and ordinary days.
Fifty-five years old and home for a visit,

back in the cradle
of his slow kind hands.

SUCH A BLUE

I sit down beside my elderly father,
quietly clasp his hand, cross
and then uncross my legs.
Long flight to get here, long
battle with emphysema and
an overworked heart for him.
The hospital door that swings
both ways for me, obdurately
keeps a good soldier in.

Not close enough, this chair,
and impossible for us to hug,
dear dad tied down—
tubes coming and going.
All a man can do to break free
is look out the window,
so I do too, and with him
simply breathe in the blue
of a cloudless sky,

"scattered light," science says,
that our eyes make into
an unrippled sea—but
there's never been such a blue
falling through me, so endless
a promise of *more*—
slowly it fills the room,
steadies the listing boat
neaped on a perilous shore.

AFTER A HEALTH SCARE
after Cecilia Woloch's "Blazon"

Him I love, with hair like saltmeadow rush,
eyes that beach me on unexpected shores,
mouth of a wild and generous sea

Under whose spell children have flown
to the moon, from whose lips the secret
lives of teddy bears told

In whose hammock of shoulders my heart swings,
his moonlit back a white bench, buttocks smooth
as ancient boulders

In whose countries of hands I am born again,
whose tongue is both midwife and stirring
anthem

Him I love, whose ticklish feet like gold bricks bank
on never being touched, legs of a mustang,
rain in the wind

In whom has lived the grip, the gale, the gall
of a thing, who as the world turns
is my world turning

Upon whose sun-blessed chest I lay my head,
hear the hammering, thank again the small
gods at work in their chambers

JANE KENYON LIVES AGAIN

as an abstract painter in my neighbourhood,
"Yielding to Transience" the theme of her
current exhibition, according to the pamphlet.
It's that simple, the only life we have we'll lose
in a neon nose dive or the drift of gradual surrender.

My Jane, who briefly entered and briefly spoke
in poems—having it out with melancholy—
said *Let evening come* and it did, under cover
of leukemia, far too soon. Wish it were otherwise.
A moody harvest, those notes from the other side.

Now there'll be a conflux of Janes when I see
one's art, read the other's poem. A conjuration—
open sesame into the chambers of two hearts.
The amazing echoes, bone's signature marrow
waving its wand again, sweet Om on the tongue.

DATE NIGHT

Often my husband and I meet for dinner at a busy restaurant.
I'll ride the bus so we can drive home together in his truck.

Whoever's there first grabs a couple of seats at the bar,
orders two glasses of Malbec, sips one and waits.

I like to think that's how it'll be in the afterlife—

one a little behind the other, the door opening
into the hum of an obviously popular place.

Zigzagging through the crowd—that glad spark
of recognition, both of us brimming with news.

ADDITIONAL ACKNOWLEDGMENTS

Behind all the words are the many people who helped make this little book happen. Particular thanks:

to Stewart Burnett, my rock, for his savvy and firm encouragement
to Wilf Burnett, for his love and giving me a beautiful den and hours to write
to David and Theresa Burnett, for their love and interest
to my parents, Barb and Jim MacFarlane, who taught me so much
to Kim Kolinsky, my soul sister, for the special pen and the good vibes and vision
to Helen Hardisty, whose heart is a river, for first giving my poems a public platform
to Susan Gough, a friend like no other
to Jeffrey Levine, Veronica Golos and the Truchas Mighty-Niners, for ongoing support and mentorship
to my six-pack—moms who've cheered each other on for 25 years now
to Jim, June, Jean, and my large extended family, for always asking about my poems

Big thanks to Leah Maines for accepting this manuscript with such enthusiasm, and to Finishing Line Press editors Kevin Maines and Christen Kincaid for their expertise and care in the book's creation.

Lynne Burnett's poems have appeared in *Blue Heron Review, Calyx, CV2, Geist, IthacaLit, Malahat Review, Modern Haiku, New Millennium Writings, North Shore Magazine, Pandora's Collective, Pedestal, Tamsen* and *Taos Journal of International Poetry & Art*, as well as three anthologies: a Tupelo Press chapbook, *On Broken Stones, New Millennium Writings* 25th Anthology and an Origami Poems Project, *The Best of Kindness 2017*. She has been shortlisted for both Arc's and New Letters' Poem of the Year, the *Malahat Review's* Far Horizons Award and three times for the Bridport Prize. She is the 2016 winner of the Lauren K. Alleyne Difficult Fruit Poetry Prize.

She lives with her husband at the foot of a mountain a block from the sea in the Pacific Northwest. Visit her blog Poems and Ponderings at https://lynneburnett.ca/